Heinemann active maths

Pupil Book 2
Addition and Subtraction

Authors: Peter Gorrie, Lynda Keith, Lynne McClure, Amy Sinclair

How to use this book

Contents

AS1.4c	Counting	3–6
AS1.5	Addition and subtraction facts	7
AS1.7a	Adding and subtracting using a 100 square	8–11
AS1.7b	Adding and subtracting using an empty number line	12
AS1.7c	Adding and subtracting using partitioning	13
AS1.8a	Adding several numbers	14–17
AS1.8b	Addition/subtraction: 1- and 2-digit numbers	18–20
AS1.8c	Addition/subtraction: 2-digit numbers	21–23
AS1.8d	Addition/subtraction: multiples of 10 and 100	24–27
AS1.9a	Adding 2-digit numbers using written methods	28
AS1.9b	Adding 2- and 3-digit numbers using written methods	29–32
AS1.10a	Subtracting 2-digit numbers using written methods	33
AS1.10b	Subtracting 2- and 3-digit numbers using written methods	34–37
AS1.11	Using the best strategy for adding and subtracting	38–40

Instructions look like this. Always read these carefully before starting.

These are Rocket activities. Ask your teacher if you need to do these questions.

Each page has a title telling you what it is about.

This shows you how to set out your work.

Read this to check you understand what you have been learning on the page.

Counting on in 11s

ASI.4c

A car race is 8 laps. Each lap is 11 kilometres.
Each car has already gone a short distance. How many kilometres will these cars have travelled by the end of each lap?

1. 2, 13, 24, 35, 46, 57, 68, 79, 90

1 2 km

2 3 km

3 6 km

4 8 km

5 12 km

6 16 km

For q1 keep adding 11 until you reach 211. Add the digits in each number. For example 24 gives 2 + 4 = 6. What do you notice about the totals?

7. Mr Howell uses 11 apples to bake a pie. He started with 85 apples. How many pies has he made when he has 19 apples left? Count back in 11s to find out.

8. Andrew is saving for an MP3 player. He starts with £64. He saves £11 a week. How many weeks until he can buy an MP3 player which costs £163?

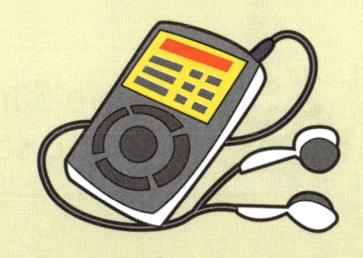

I can count on and back in 11s

Counting in 50s

ASI.4c

Each bag holds 50 tacks. How many tacks?

1. 150

1 2 3 4

5 6 7 8

9 Copy and complete the table.

Number of bags	10	15		18		22	17	
Number of tacks			650		350			1950

10

A young bird weighs 42 g.

It gains 50 g every week.

What is the bird's weight after 8 weeks?

I save 50p each week. About how many years will it take to save £1000? Use a calculator to help.

I can count in 50s

4

Counting in 25s and 50s

ASI.4c

1. Copy and complete the table.

	600	705	725	1005	810	100	48	130	350	950	425
In 50s count	✓										
In 25s count	✓										

2. When you add the digits of the numbers in the 50s count, you get a pattern. What is the pattern? Start from 50.

$$250 \quad 2 + 5 + 0 = 7$$
$$300 \quad 3 + 0 + 0 = 3$$
$$350 \quad 3 + 5 + 0 = 8$$

What pattern do you notice if you add the digits of the numbers in the 25s count?

Write the next three numbers in the count.

3. 75, 100, 125

3. 0, 25, 50
4. 150, 175, 200
5. 275, 300, 325
6. 75, 100, 125
7. 50, 75, 100
8. 200, 225, 250

9. Sandy has a savings account. Every week she pays in £50. She starts with £300. How many weeks until she has £1000?

10. A water tower leaks 50 l a day. It has 2000 l. How long before it runs dry?

I can count in 25s and 50s

5

Counting in 25s

ASI.4c

1. Felix is too thin! | He eats more. | He gains 25g each week. | He does this for a year. | How much weight has he gained?

Start counting on from 32. Count in 25s. What is the tenth number? Look at the patterns. Can you predict the 100th number?

There is 25 cm between each rung. The painter steps down one rung at a time. Write the height he will be at on each rung until he reaches the bottom of the ladder.

2. 59 cm, 34 cm, 9 cm

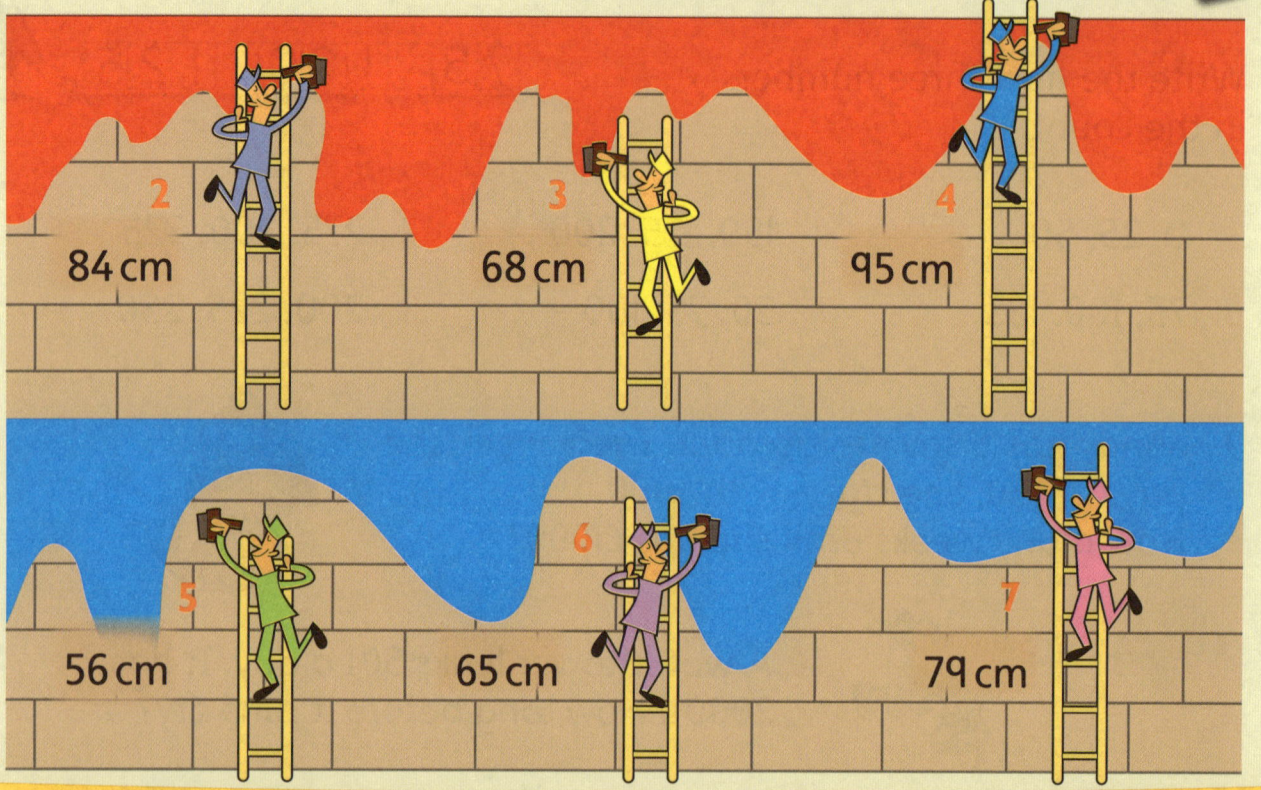

2. 84 cm
3. 68 cm
4. 95 cm
5. 56 cm
6. 65 cm
7. 79 cm

I can count in 25s

Addition and subtraction facts

1. John knows that 4 + 3 = 7. Show three other number facts using the digits 7, 3 and 4.

2. Ed wants to solve 500 + 200. His teacher tells him that he knows an easier calculation that will help.
   What is the easier calculation? Use it to find the answer.

3. Sally is making a pattern. Copy and complete the pattern.

   8 – 5 = 3
   18 – 5 = ___
   28 – 5 = ___
   _____
   _____
   58 – 5 = ___

4. Shona uses Sally's pattern to make another pattern. Copy and complete Shona's pattern.

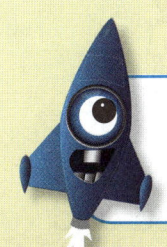

   3 + 5 = 8
   13 + 5 = ___
   _____
   _____
   _____
   53 + 5 = ___

What number facts can you work out when you know that 6 + 7 = 13?

I can use the addition and subtraction facts that I know to work out new facts

ASI.7a

Number pairs to 100

Each box held 100 marbles. How many have been lost?

1. $100 - 64 = 36$

1. 64
2. 72
3. 54
4. 38
5. 57
6. 69
7. 52
8. 67
9. 35

Can you find two 2-digit numbers that add to 100 and whose four digits do not add to 19? What is the rule for those that do not add to 19?

10. Sunil has 100 conkers. He gives 34 to his younger sister. How many does he have left?

11. Mrs Sums has 100 stickers. She uses 27 in an assembly. How many does she have left?

12. Tom pays 36p for his ice-cream, using a £1 coin. How much change does he have? Suppose he buys two ice-creams?

13. There are 100 pens in a box. 47 are red and the rest are blue. How many are blue?

I know pairs that add together to make 100

Adding

How old will each parrot be?

1. 36 years, lives 23 more years
2. 54 years, lives 24 more years
3. 67 years, lives 21 more years
4. 72 years, lives 27 more years
5. 53 years, lives 44 more years
6. 65 years, lives 25 more years

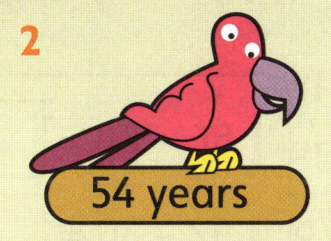

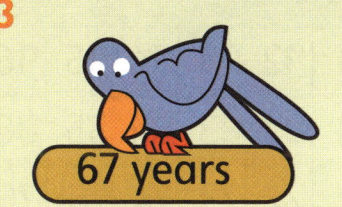

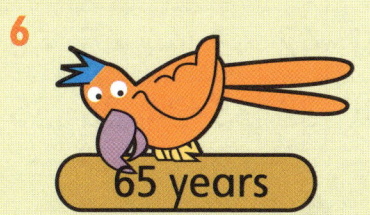

Complete these additions using your 100-square.

7. 48 + 36 =
8. 55 + 37 =
9. 56 + 36 =
10. 39 + 44 =
11. 57 + 26 =
12. 42 + 38 =

13. Jim has £54. His brother has saved £38. They want to buy a bike for £100. How much more must they save?

Find pairs of numbers that add to 100 where all four digits are different.

I can add pairs of 2-digit numbers

ASI.7a

Subtracting multiples of 10

Copy and complete. Use a 100-square to help.

1. 86 − 50 = 36

90	91	92	93	94	95	96	97	98
80	81	82	83	84	85	86	87	88
70	71	72	73	74	75	76	77	78
60	61	62	63	64	65	66	67	68
50	51	52	53	54	55	56	57	58
40	41	42	43	44	45	46	47	48
30	31	32	33	34	35	36	37	38

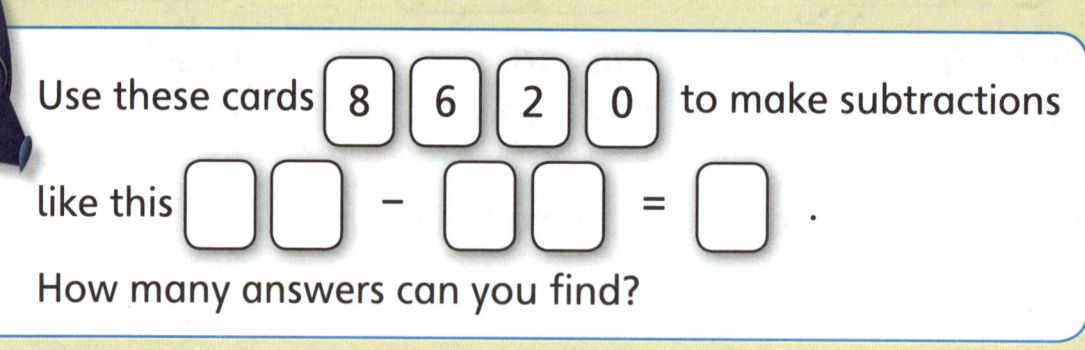

1 86 − 50 =
2 75 − 20 =
3 92 − 30 =
4 66 − 40 =
5 85 − 60 =
6 71 − 50 =
7 36 − 10 =
8 47 − 20 =
9 78 − 40 =
10 55 − 40 =

Use these cards 8 6 2 0 to make subtractions like this ☐☐ − ☐☐ = ☐ .
How many answers can you find?

11 Fiona has 74 marbles. She gives 30 marbles to Ella. How many marbles does Fiona have left?

12 Catherine has 52 football cards. She gives her brother Struan 40 cards. How many cards does Catherine have left?

13 John has 92 pennies in a jar. He spends 50 of them. How many pennies does John have left?

I can subtract multiples of 10 from 2-digit numbers

Addition and subtraction facts

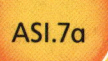

ASI.7a

Use the number square to copy and complete the subtractions.

91	92	93	94	95	96	97	98	99	100
81	82	83	84	85	86	87	88	89	90
71	72	73	74	75	76	77	78	79	80
61	62	63	64	65	66	67	68	69	70
51	52	53	54	55	56	57	58	59	60
41	42	43	44	45	46	47	48	49	50
31	32	33	34	35	36	37	38	39	40
21	22	23	24	25	26	27	28	29	30
11	12	13	14	15	16	17	18	19	20
1	2	3	4	5	6	7	8	9	10

1. 50 − 18 = 32

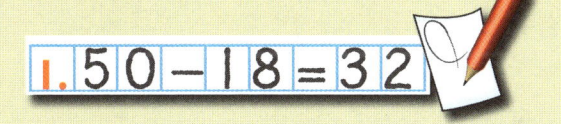

1. 50 − ☐ = 32
2. 70 − ☐ = 52
3. 67 − ☐ = 24
4. 53 − ☐ = 29
5. 28 = 74 − ☐
6. 45 = 78 − ☐
7. 51 = 96 − ☐
8. 62 = 91 − ☐
9. 74 = 99 − ☐
10. 18 = 46 − ☐
11. 14 = 78 − ☐
12. 75 = 101 − ☐

13. James has 74 marbles in a box. His brother Callum takes some out. 58 marbles are left in the box. How many marbles did Callum take?

14. Stuart has 56 books on his bookshelf. He gives some books to Lorna. Stuart has 28 books left. How many books did he give to Lorna?

I can subtract using a 100-square to help me

Adding and subtracting

Copy and complete.

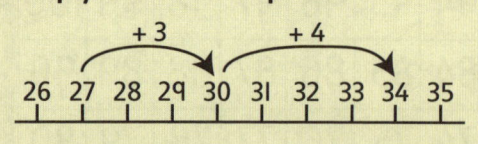

1. ☐2☐7☐+☐7☐=☐3☐4☐

```
      +3      +4
    ⌒      ⌒
26 27 28 29 30 31 32 33 34 35
```

1 27 + 7 =
     /\
    3 + 4

```
       +6       +2
     ⌒       ⌒
82 83 84 85 86 87 88 89 90 91 92 93 94
```

2 84 + 8 =
     /\
    6 + 2

```
44 45 46 47 48 49 50 51 52 53 54 55 56 57 58 59
```

3 47 + 6 =

4 55 – 8 =

```
      54           60                    70
```

5 54 + 8 =

6 65 – 7 =

```
73                                              44
```

7 73 + 8 =

8 44 – 5 =

Use an empty number line to find the answer.

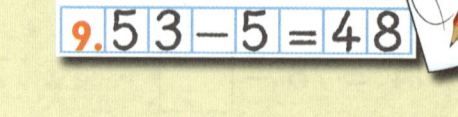

9. ☐5☐3☐–☐5☐=☐4☐8☐

```
                     –2   –3
                    ⌒   ⌒
    40              48  50  53              60
```

9 53 – 5 =

10 46 + 7 =

11 37 + 6 =

12 52 – 8 =

13 38 – 4 =

14 45 + 6 =

Adding an even number to another number can give an even answer. When is this true?

I can use an empty number line to help with adding and subtracting

Adding 2-digit numbers

Add the tens and units card numbers.

1. 47 + 36 = 40 + 30 + 7 + 6 = 70 + 13 = 83

1. 40 7 / 30 6
2. 50 2 / 40 8
3. 20 3 / 40 9
4. 70 8 / 10 7
5. 60 3 / 40 8
6. 30 6 / 20 7
7. 50 3 / 60 6
8. 40 5 / 70 4
9. 30 3 / 50 7

Add the prices.

10. 48p + 67p = 115p

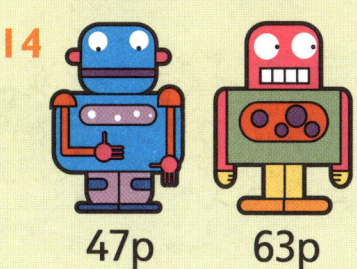

10. 48p 67p
11. 74p 65p
12. 81p 49p
13. 56p 72p
14. 47p 63p
15. 63p 59p

Two numbers add to make 121. Each number has both digits the same. What could the numbers be?

I can add 2-digit numbers using tens and units

Adding several numbers

Find each total score!

1. 8, 9, 6, 2
2. 8, 3, 8, 7
3. 4, 6, 9, 6
4. 9, 9, 1, 4
5. 6, 3, 7, 5
6. 5, 4, 5, 3

I've got four cards from a normal pack. I have no picture cards. My score is 25. What could my cards be?

7. 11p + 5p + 9p + 3p = 28p

Write how much for each snack. Look for pairs to 20.

7. 11p, 5p, 9p, 3p
8. 12p, 2p, 5p, 8p
9. 2p, 14p, 8p, 6p
10. 5p, 15p, 6p, 8p
11. 3p, 6p, 17p, 4p
12. 3p, 16p, 8p, 5p

I can add several numbers and find the total

Adding several numbers

ASI.8a

Find the total time for each child's tasks.

1. $8 + 2 + 5 + 3 = 18$ minutes
   10

How can you make these calculations easier?

1. Clear table: 3 minutes
   Wash up: 8 minutes
   Dry up: 5 minutes
   Put cutlery away: 2 minutes

2. Feed dog: 6 minutes
   Let dog out: 7 minutes
   Tidy up dog bowls: 4 minutes
   Brush dog: 8 minutes

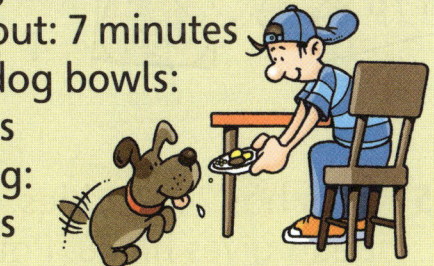

3. Find school bag: 5 minutes
   Do homework: 9 minutes
   Find gym kit: 5 minutes
   Pack gym bag: 6 minutes
   Make sandwiches: 9 minutes

4. Make bed: 3 minutes
   Tidy toys: 3 minutes
   Dust shelves: 4 minutes
   Clean shoes: 9 minutes
   Put away clothes: 7 minutes

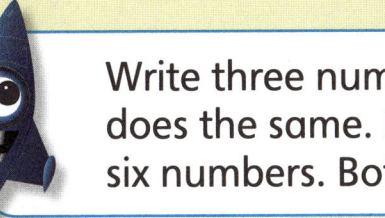

Write three numbers between 2 and 10. Your partner does the same. Both guess the answer if you add all six numbers. Both do the addition. Who was closest?

Add the card numbers.

5. $30 + 70 + 80 + 40 = 220$

How can you make these calculations easier?

5. 40 70 80 30
6. 50 60 50 80
7. 60 70 70 40
8. 80 70 40 20 30
9. 70 10 90 90
10. 70 60 90 30
11. 80 60 90 20
12. 60 80 50 40

I can add more than two numbers and find the total

15

Adding several numbers

Add the ticket amounts.

1. $22p + 10p + 9p = 41p$

1. 9p, 7p, 3p, 22p
2. 2p, 12p, 9p, 35p, 8p
3. 26p, 8p, 9p, 1p, 4p
4. 6p, 4p, 1p, 7p, 5p

5. Sam has 24 marbles. Asif gives him 9 marbles, Bella gives him 8, Paul gives him 4 and he finds 3 more. How many does he have now? How many more does he need to make 50?

23 roses   9 roses   3 roses   7 roses

6. Roses are £2 each. How much money do you need to buy all the roses?

7. Choose five objects. Add the prices. Do this six times. Record your answers.

4p, 19p, 6p, 8p, 2p, 17p, 3p
14p, 9p, 12p, 11p, 7p, 5p, 15p, 5p

I have no 1p or 2p coins. Which amounts between 1p and 50p can I not make?

I can add several numbers and find the total

Adding several numbers

Find the total cost of each set of stamps.

1. 22p + 8p + 3p + 7p + 9p = 49p

1. 7p, 3p, 8p, 9p, 22p
2. 9p, 17p, 6p, 4p, 8p
3. 17p, 5p, 24p, 19p, 3p
4. 2p, 25p, 9p, 8p, 24p
5. 4p, 27p, 3p, 16p, 4p
6. 7p, 21p, 19p, 14p, 2p
7. 25p, 8p, 4p, 25p, 9p
8. 27p, 8p, 4p, 7p, 3p, 5p
9. 6p, 27p, 4p, 9p, 2p
10. 24p, 9p, 6p, 17p, 3p
11. 18p, 9p, 8p, 4p, 23p
12. 5p, 8p, 23p, 18p, 4p

13. You are in charge of the Post Office! You sell stamps with five different values, e.g. 1p, 2p, 5p, 10p, 20p.

Use as few of your stamps as possible to make each total from questions 1 to 12.

I can add more than two numbers and find the total

Adding and subtracting

ASI.8b

Copy and complete.
Use a number grid to help.

1. 56 + 9 = 65

1 56 + 9 = ☐   2 27 + 9 = ☐   3 38 + 9 = ☐

4 65 + 9 = ☐   5 73 + 9 = ☐   6 46 + 9 = ☐

Now try these!

7 27 + 11 = ☐   8 43 + 11 = ☐   9 28 + 11 = ☐

Each price is reduced by 9p.
Write the new prices.

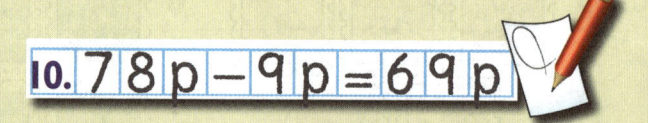

10. 78p – 9p = 69p

10 78p
11 65p
12 87p
13 56p
14 42p
15 64p
16 92p
17 85p
18 54p
19 43p

The prices should have actually gone up by 9p. Write the correct prices.

How many times can you take away 9 from 99?

I can add and subtract numbers

Adding and subtracting

Copy and complete.

1. $24 + 19 = 43$

1. $24 + 19 = \square$
2. $42 + 19 = \square$
3. $48 + 19 = \square$
4. $63 + 21 = \square$
5. $36 + 21 = \square$
6. $72 + 21 = \square$

True or false?

7. To subtract 19, you take away 20, then take away 1 more.

8. To add 39, you add 40 then add 1 more.

9. 21 less than a number is the same as 9 more than 30 less than a number.

How much is left after the ticket has been bought?

10. $£46 - £19 = £27$

10. £46, ticket: £19
11. £42, ticket: £19
12. £38, ticket: £19
13. £56, ticket: £21
14. £64, ticket: £21
15. £88, ticket: £21

Choose a 2-digit number with all the digits the same, e.g. 11, 22 or 33. Add and subtract 19. Compare the units. What do you notice?

I can add and subtract numbers

Adding and subtracting

Copy and complete.

1. 354 + 39 = 393

| 1 | 354 + 39 = ☐ | 2 | 327 + 49 = ☐ | 3 | 312 + 29 = ☐ |
| 4 | 332 + 29 = ☐ | 5 | 325 + 59 = ☐ | 6 | 443 + 39 = ☐ |

7. Sid Seal is fed 250 tiny fish each day.

7. 250 − 29 = 221

Monday	Leaves 29
Tuesday	Leaves 41
Wednesday	Leaves 99
Thursday	Leaves 19
Friday	Leaves 39
Saturday	Leaves 59
Sunday	Leaves 119

How many does he eat each day?

How many fish are not eaten altogether?

Write the new prices.

8. £582 − £39 = £543

BIKE SALE

| 8 | £582 £39 off | 9 | £476 £29 off | 10 | £553 £31 off | 11 | £397 £51 off |

How many times can you subtract 59 from 1000? Estimate first!

I can add and subtract 2- and 3-digit numbers

Adding

Copy and complete. How did you find your answer?

1. 36 + 23 = ☐
2. 36 + 42 = ☐
3. 42 + 33 = ☐
4. 45 + 34 = ☐
5. 17 + 42 = ☐
6. 32 + 12 = ☐
7. 51 + 25 = ☐
8. 28 + 91 = ☐

9. Choose two items. Add them. Write the total.

- £39
- £48
- £18
- £27
- £19
- £25
- £49
- £28
- £53

Find two numbers which can be added to give 51. Both numbers must have a units digit greater than or equal to 5.

I can add 2-digit numbers

Adding

Copy and complete. How did you find your answer?

1. 374 + 268 =
2. 286 + 418 =
3. 375 + 188 =
4. 278 + 187 =
5. 392 + 129 =
6. 188 + 276 =
7. 283 + 379 =
8. 235 + 566 =

9. C A T + D O G = R O W

Each letter represents a digit.
No digit is represented by more than one letter.
Write the sum in numbers.
Hint: O = 1. Use number cards to help.

Both these people received their telegram from the Queen. They were over 100 when they died! Write the year they died.

10. Granny Eliza was born in 1900 and got married aged 28. Then she was a village shopkeeper for 46 years. She was retired for 27 years.

11. Grandpa Will was born in 1898 and got married aged 28. After that he was a postman for 45 years, and then lived in retirement for 28 years.

I can add 2- and 3-digit numbers

Subtracting

ASI.8c

How tall is each bush after being cut?

1. 8 2 − 1 8 = 6 4 cm

1 82 cm 18 cm cut
2 73 cm 36 cm cut
3 94 cm 25 cm cut
4 65 cm 28 cm cut
5 71 cm 27 cm cut
6 63 cm 15 cm cut
7 208 cm 32 cm cut
8 183 cm 58 cm cut
9 274 cm 37 cm cut

Draw your own bush and write its height.
Write a subtraction to cut it in half. Keep going.

Choose the largest and the smallest number.
Find the difference between them.

10 183 47
11 188 221
12 144 86
13 164 55
14 187 214
15 136 372

I can subtract 2- and 3-digit numbers

23

Multiples of 10

Copy and complete.

1. $14 - 6 = 8$
   $140 - 60 = 80$

1. $14 - 6 = \square$
   $140 - 60 = \square$

2. $17 + 5 = \square$
   $170 + 50 = \square$

3. $16 - 7 = \square$
   $160 - 70 = \square$

4. $24 + 8 = \square$
   $240 + 80 = \square$

5. $12 - 5 = \square$
   $120 - 50 = \square$

6. $17 + 9 = \square$
   $170 + 90 = \square$

7. $18 + 7 = \square$
   $180 + 70 = \square$

8. $13 - 7 = \square$
   $130 - 70 = \square$

9. $15 - 8 = \square$
   $150 - 80 = \square$

10. $23 - 9 = \square$
    $230 - 90 = \square$

11. $21 - 8 = \square$
    $210 - 80 = \square$

12. $11 - 7 = \square$
    $110 - 70 = \square$

13. Choose one red card and one yellow card.
    Find the total and the difference. Do this six times.

Red cards: 150, 320, 510, 120
Yellow cards: 50, 90, 240, 70, 60

Try adding all the red cards, then adding all the yellow cards, and finding the difference between the two totals.

I can add and subtract multiples of 10

Multiples of 10

Find the total crowd at each concert.
Find the difference between the numbers of adults and children.

1. 310 + 70 = 380
   310 − 70 = 240

1 310 adults, 70 children

2 220 adults, 70 children
3 440 adults, 80 children
4 230 adults, 90 children
5 340 adults, 60 children
6 150 adults, 80 children
7 210 adults, 80 children

Tickets cost £10 for adults and £5 for children. How much does each concert make?

Copy and complete.

8. 320 − 60 = 260

8 320 − 60 =
9 430 − 80 =
10 370 + 70 =
11 360 + 80 =
12 880 + 40 =
13 830 − 60 =
14 710 − 90 =
15 280 + 50 =
16 640 + 50 =

I can add and subtract multiples of 10

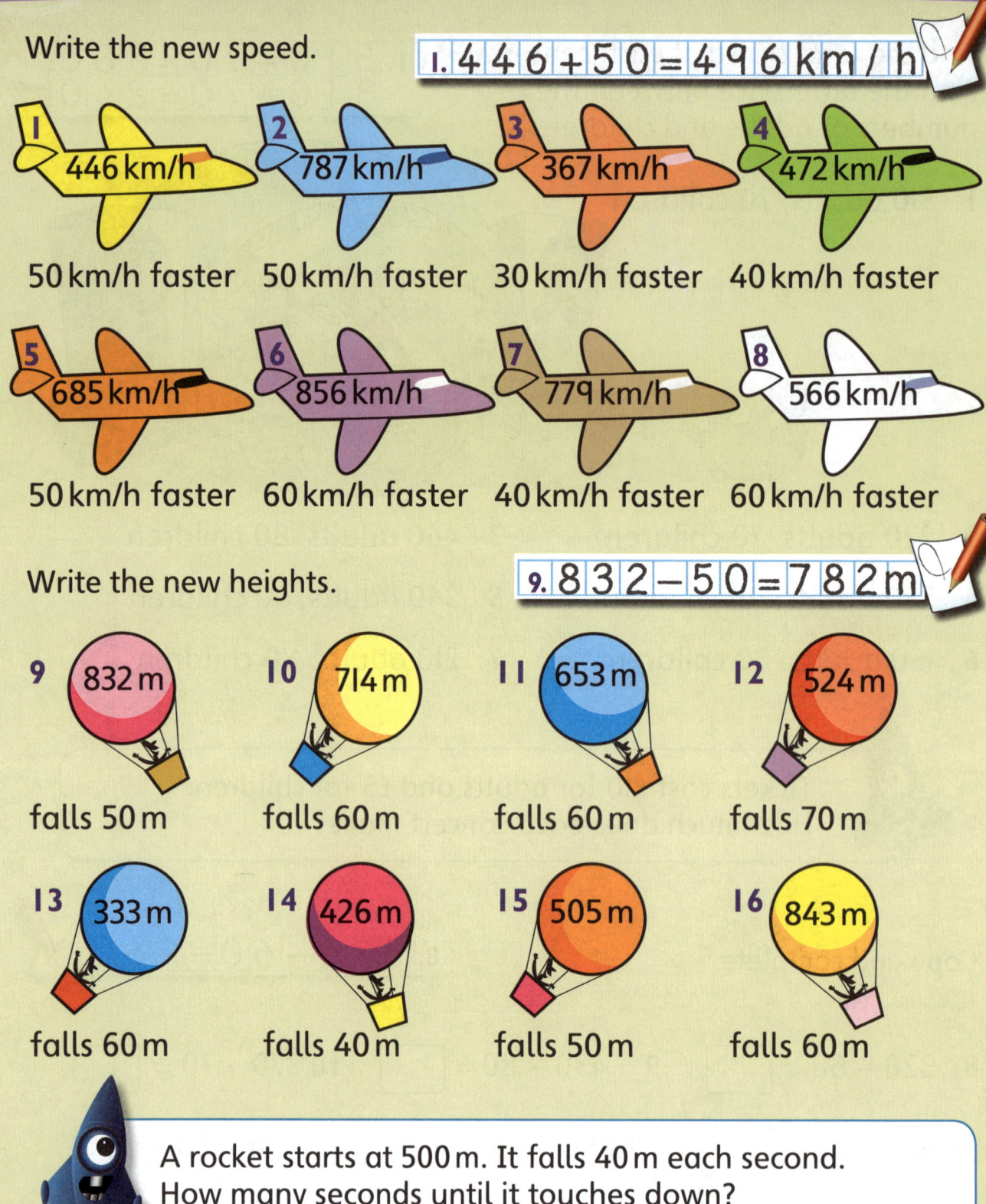

Multiples of 10

Write the new speed.

1. $446 + 50 = 496$ km/h

1. 446 km/h — 50 km/h faster
2. 787 km/h — 50 km/h faster
3. 367 km/h — 30 km/h faster
4. 472 km/h — 40 km/h faster
5. 685 km/h — 50 km/h faster
6. 856 km/h — 60 km/h faster
7. 779 km/h — 40 km/h faster
8. 566 km/h — 60 km/h faster

Write the new heights.

9. $832 - 50 = 782$ m

9. 832 m falls 50 m
10. 714 m falls 60 m
11. 653 m falls 60 m
12. 524 m falls 70 m
13. 333 m falls 60 m
14. 426 m falls 40 m
15. 505 m falls 50 m
16. 843 m falls 60 m

A rocket starts at 500 m. It falls 40 m each second. How many seconds until it touches down? Make up a rocket landing problem for your partner to solve.

I can add and subtract multiples of 10 to and from other numbers

Multiples of 100

Write each climber's new height.

1. 8400 − 300 = 8100 m

1. 8400 m climbs down 300 m
2. 7800 m climbs down 400 m
3. 7500 m climbs down 500 m
4. 6900 m climbs down 500 m
5. 6400 m climbs down 200 m
6. 5800 m climbs down 300 m

Each climber was sponsored to climb the mountain. Add the two cheques.

7. £2700 + £500 = £3200

7. £2700   £500
8. £4500   £600
9. £3600   £800
10. £5800   £500

I start at 1500 m. I climb down in multiples of 100 m, but I never climb down more than 400 m at any one time. How many ways of getting to the ground are there?

I can add and subtract multiples of 100

Number pairs

How much will the two lollies cost?

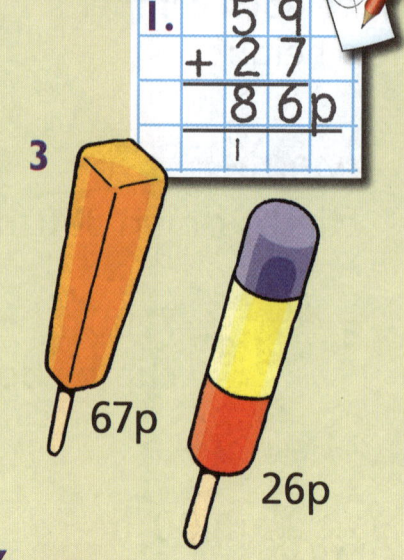

$$\begin{array}{r} 1. 59 \\ +27 \\ \hline 86p \\ {}^1 \end{array}$$

1 59p   27p
2 68p   18p
3 67p   26p
4 35p   57p
5 33p   44p
6 35p   67p

Copy and complete.

7   36   8   56   9   42
   +77   +27   +89
   ___   ___   ___

10 35   11 73   12 56
   +97   +47   +56
   ___   ___   ___

$$\begin{array}{r} 7. 36 \\ +77 \\ \hline 113 \\ {}^1 \end{array}$$

Make up four calculations for your partner.

I can add 2-digit numbers by writing one under the other

Adding

Each donkey is carrying a rider and two saddlebags. How much weight in total?

```
1.  H T U
    1 2 7
      5 4
  + 1 1 5
    2 9 6
      1
```

1 Rider: 127 kg
Bag 1: 54 kg
Bag 2: 115 kg

2 Rider: 128 kg
Bag 1: 110 kg
Bag 2: 36 kg

3 Rider: 112 kg
Bag 1: 73 kg
Bag 2: 23 kg

4 Rider: 109 kg
Bag 1: 57 kg
Bag 2: 85 kg

Using these cards: 1 2 3 4 5 6 7 8 9

in order, what is the answer to this addition?

☐☐ + ☐☐☐ + ☐☐☐☐

Try in reverse order.

5 Addy drives 128 miles to see his mum. He then drives 26 miles to the beach, and 147 miles home. How far has he driven?

6 It is 128 days until Christmas. Then it is 43 days until Lucy's birthday. Then it is 54 days until her big holiday! How long to wait?

Add some 3-digit numbers to make exactly 1000. Can you do this in several different ways?

I can add 2- and 3-digit numbers by writing one under the other

Adding

How many grams of gold does each pair of gold diggers have in total? First write your estimate.

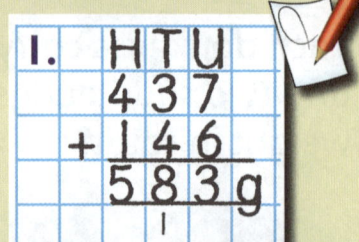

```
1.  H T U
    4 3 7
  + 1 4 6
    5 8 3 g
      1
```

1 146 g 437 g

2 378 g 166 g

3 526 g 219 g

4 176 g 359 g

5 468 g 129 g

6 336 g 158 g

7 Choose two water pouches. Write an approximate total. Work out the addition. Repeat six times.

342 ml 686 ml 455 ml 548 ml 189 ml

Work with a partner to find ways of using the digits 1 2 3 4 5 6 7 to make this addition work:

☐☐☐ + ☐☐☐ = ☐ 0 0

I can add 3-digit numbers by writing one under the other

Adding

Each child does three jumps. Find the total length. Round each jump to the nearest 10 cm and use this to find the approximate total length.

1. 167 cm
   72 cm
   86 cm

2. 154 cm
   65 cm
   23 cm

3. 175 cm
   54 cm
   38 cm

4. 165 cm
   38 cm
   46 cm

1. Calculation
```
  1 6 7
    7 2
+   8 6
-------
  3 2 5 cm
    2 1
```

Rounding
```
  1 7 0
    7 0
+   9 0
-------
  3 3 0 cm
    2
```

Work with a partner. Use the digits 1 2 3 4 5 6 7 to get the largest possible total from this addition:

☐☐ + ☐☐ + ☐☐ =

5. Omar drives 285 miles to London and a further 126 miles to Bristol. He then drives 168 miles to Cornwall. How far does he drive in total?

6. Emma's puppy is 1 year and 85 days old today. How many days has she lived? If she was born on 1st January, what is today's date?

7. Annie has weighed her ingredients. She has 864 g of flour and 275 g of sugar. She adds 189 g of butter. What is the total weight?

I can add several 2- and 3-digit numbers by writing them one under the other

Adding

1. Choose three videos. Estimate the total running time in minutes. Add the numbers and work it out. Repeat six times.

FILL BILL — 126 minutes

SIT BY ME — 98 minutes

JAMES POND — 87 minutes

101 Labradors — 119 minutes

sleeping ugly — 145 minutes

Shrok — 137 minutes

£368   £467   £459   £386   £555

Choose three cheques to make the largest total possible.

Write your estimate first, then do the addition.

Now choose the three cheques that give the second largest total.

Repeat this to find the five highest possible totals.

Now repeat this to find the five lowest possible totals.

Write the ten different cheque totals in order, largest to smallest.

I can add several 2- and 3-digit numbers by writing them one under the other

Subtracting

Copy and complete.

1.
```
      6 1      6 1
  7 3    7 3    7 3
- 4 7  - 4 7  - 4 7
              6   2 6
```

1. 73
   − 47
   ____

2. 61
   − 43
   ____

3. 82
   − 58
   ____

4. 71
   − 38
   ____

5. 62
   − 27
   ____

6. 74
   − 46
   ____

Write two numbers whose difference is equal to the smaller number. Do this six times. What do you notice?

7 Choose two numbers. Subtract the smaller from the larger. Do this six times.

74   38   82   65   57

I can subtract 2-digit numbers by writing one under the other

Subtracting

ASI.10b

Copy and complete.

1	346 − 84	2	248 − 73	3	126 − 62	4	482 − 76
5	335 − 82	6	137 − 85	7	227 − 64	8	124 − 86

$$\begin{array}{r} \overset{2\;1}{\cancel{3}46} \\ -\;\;84 \\ \hline 262 \end{array}$$

Choose a subtraction you found hard. With a partner, add the answer to the smaller number to check it.

How much further to read?

9. 146 — 261 pages in total
10. 158 — 372 pages in total
11. 165 — 481 pages in total
12. 137 — 564 pages in total
13. 128 — 473 pages in total
14. 147 — 583 pages in total

Use number cards 1–9.
Make a subtraction like this: ☐☐☐ − ☐☐☐
Complete the subtraction. Check by adding.

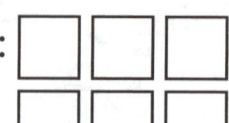

I can subtract 2- and 3-digit numbers by writing one under the other

Subtracting

Copy and complete.

1. 354
    − 167
    ─────

2. 423
    − 176
    ─────

3. 524
    − 178
    ─────

4. 325
    − 158
    ─────

5. 436
    − 187
    ─────

6. 341
    − 174
    ─────

1. $\overset{2}{3}\overset{4}{5}\overset{1}{4}$
    − 1 6 7
    ─────
    1 8 7

This is Tim's homework. He got some subtractions wrong. Where did he make the errors?

7. $4\overset{2}{3}\overset{1}{7}$
    − 1 2 9
    ─────
    3 0 8

8. $2\overset{7}{8}\overset{1}{4}$
    − 1 3 9
    ─────
    1 4 4

9. $\overset{3}{4}\overset{0}{1}\overset{1}{6}$
    − 1 8 3
    ─────
    2 2 7

10. $\overset{5}{6}\overset{1}{3}9$
    − 2 5 4
    ─────
    3 8 5

11. 5 2 4
    − 1 8 3
    ─────
    4 1 1

12. $\overset{2}{3}\overset{3}{4}\overset{1}{1}$
    − 1 5 8
    ─────
    1 8 3

Use these cards:

| 1 | 3 | 4 | 5 | 7 | 8 |

Make a subtraction like this: ☐☐☐
                             − ☐☐☐

Find ways that give the largest answer, the smallest answer, and the answer closest to 100.

I can subtract 3-digit numbers by writing one under the other

ASI.10b

Subtracting

1. Choose a pair of numbers. Work out the difference. Repeat this to find all ten pairs.

Estimate first

1.
```
   6 10 1
   7  X  2
-  3  4  5
   3  6  7
```

Cars: 345, 179, 712, 534, 268

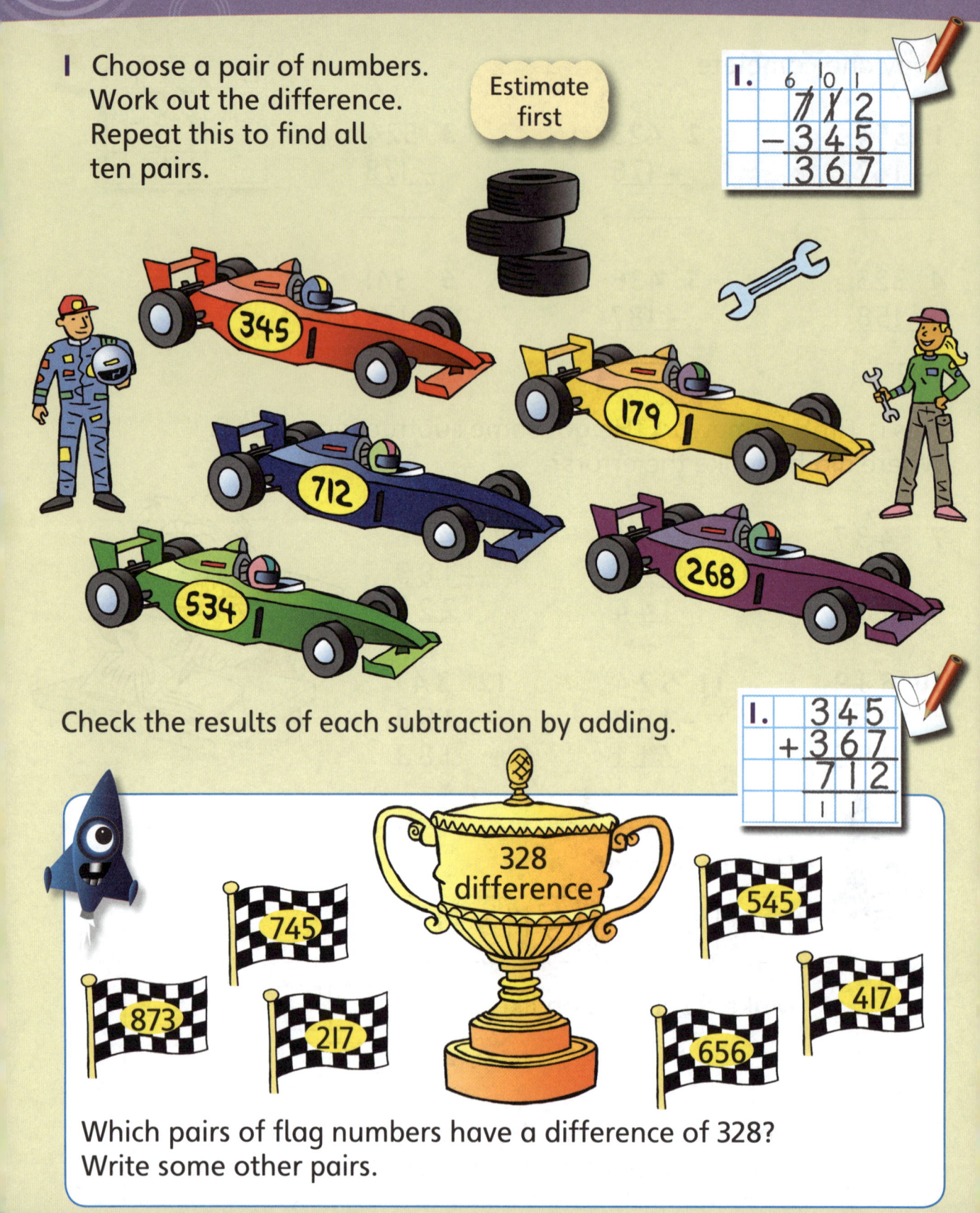

Check the results of each subtraction by adding.

1.
```
   3 4 5
 + 3 6 7
   7 1 2
   1 1
```

328 difference

Flags: 745, 545, 873, 217, 656, 417

Which pairs of flag numbers have a difference of 328? Write some other pairs.

36   I can subtract 3-digit numbers by writing one under the other

Subtracting

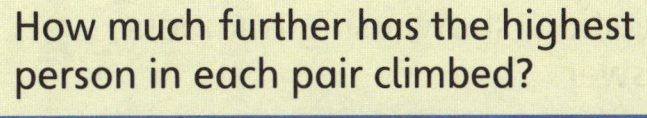

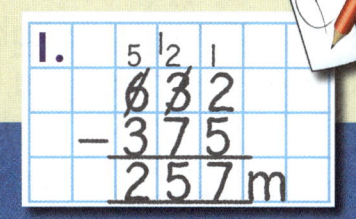

How much further has the highest person in each pair climbed?

1.
$$\begin{array}{r} {}^5\cancel{6}{}^{1}\cancel{3}2 \\ -375 \\ \hline 257\,m \end{array}$$

Copy and complete.

7 325 − 187 = ☐   8 362 − 88 = ☐   9 543 − 168 = ☐

10 525 − 377 = ☐   11 613 − 366 = ☐   12 757 − 239 = ☐

Write pairs of heights where the difference is a 3-digit number with next-door digits, e.g. 123, 234; 345 …

I can subtract 3-digit numbers by writing one under the other

37

Adding and subtracting

Write the new weight. For each question, show, using numbers and signs, how you found your answer.

1. 328 g, gains 48 g
2. 454 g, gains 38 g
3. 562 g, gains 39 g
4. 434 g, gains 57 g
5. 669 g, gains 28 g
6. 375 g, gains 22 g

7. Take a 2-digit number and reverse the digits. Take the smaller number from the larger number. Repeat this. What do you notice?

7. 34   43
   43 − 34 = 9

How much further to go?

8. 374 − 23 = 351 km

8. 374 km, driven 23 km
9. 278 km, driven 42 km
10. 165 km, driven 33 km
11. 585 km, driven 44 km
12. 294 km, driven 52 km
13. 245 km, driven 34 km

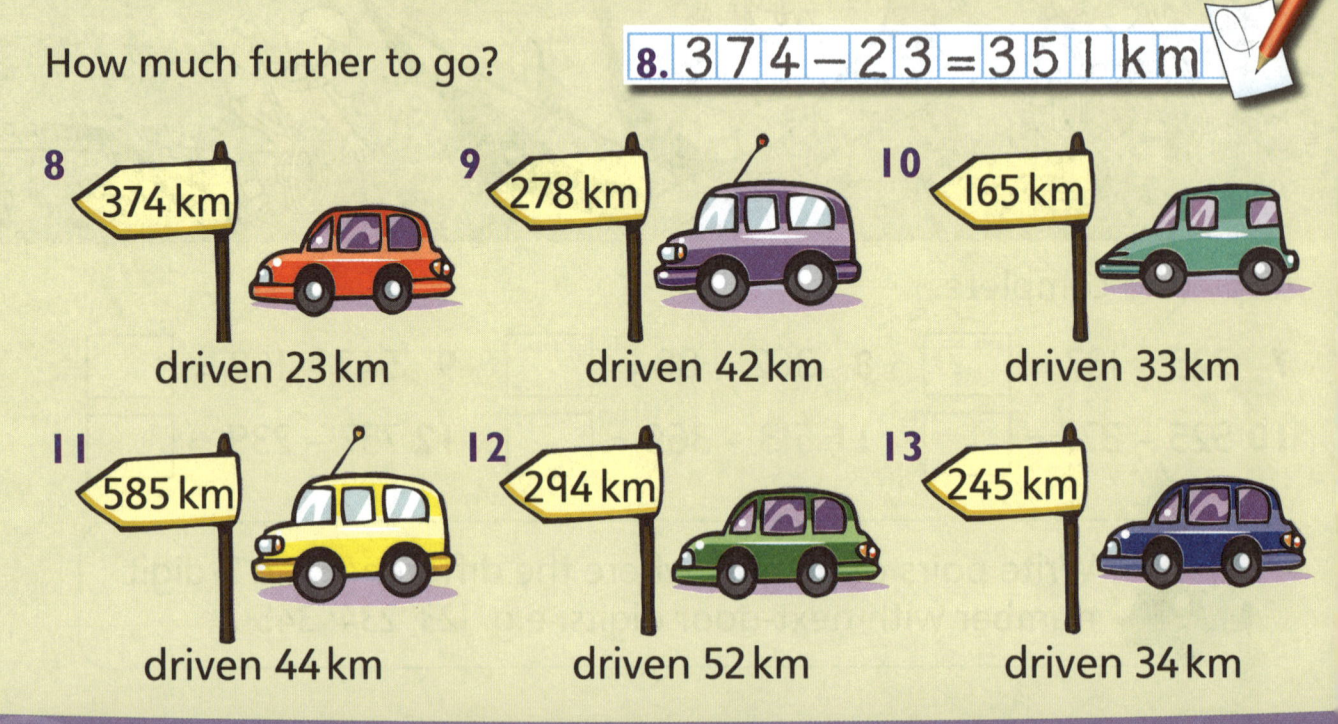

I can choose the most appropriate strategy to add and subtract

Adding and subtracting

Work out the cost of each meal.

1. £2·76 + 18p = £2·94

1. £2·76   18p
2. £3·25   28p
3. £1·75   32p
4. £2·60   15p
5. £3·85   18p
6. £2·80   15p

You are the teacher! This is Sarah's homework. Check it, and correct any wrong answers.

Be the Teacher

7. 148 − 26 = 122
8. 84 − 53 = 32
9. 92 − 43 = 49
10. 254 − 42 = 221
11. 87 − 38 = 59
12. 566 − 51 = 515
13. 839 − 27 = 812
14. 74 − 35 = 31
15. 82 − 19 = 63
16. 65 − 18 = 57

Write four subtractions. Make two of them wrong. Give them to your partner to mark.

I can choose the most appropriate strategy to add and subtract

Adding and subtracting

How many bricks now?

1. 138 bricks, 100 more
2. 125 bricks, 15 more
3. 243 bricks, 40 more
4. 176 bricks, 19 more
5. 136 bricks, 169 more
6. 217 bricks, 439 more

Copy and complete.

7. 87 − 20 =
8. 133 − 40 =
9. 256 − 120 =
10. 84 − 39 =
11. 300 − 149 =
12. 410 − 101 =

Write some subtractions like this one: 35 − 29, where the tens digit in the first number is only 1 more than the tens digit in the second number. Do the subtractions. What do you notice?

13. A film lasts 126 minutes. Jane and her dad left after 79 minutes. How much did they miss?

14. Asif has earned £193. His grandma gives him a bonus of £67. How much does he have now?

15. Chang rode 72 miles on her bike. For the last 25 miles her gears were not working. For how many miles were the gears working?

16. Tom runs 126 m from his house to the park, then runs 89 m round the park. How far does he run in total?

I can choose the appropriate strategy to add and subtract